Who *FARTED* in the Boardroom?!

Who *FARTED* in the Boardroom?

How to Outscore **CONFLICT** in the Workplace

Diara Kendrich, M.S.

Cover Design provided by:
Miguel K.

Photography provided by:
Jehan, Inc.
www.jehaninc.com

Diara Kendrich
P.O. Box 723011
Atlanta, GA 31139
Visit www.dkendrich.com

Printed in the United States of America
First Edition: March 2013

Kendrich, Diara.
    Who Farted in the Boardroom?!: How to Outscore Conflict in the Workplace / Diara Kendrich.
        ISBN: 978-1483976334

CONTENTS

INTRODUCTION

"Who FARTED in the Boardroom?!" is an awkward question that only the most daring individual would ask, and the one who admits to doing so would be considered the most outspoken and tenacious person in the room. Now, in retrospect, is admitting to this humiliating act really a bad thing? The moment it happens in the boardroom or in the presence of at least one other person can be a discommoding situation. However, the decision to speak up and admit this act represents ownership, reliability, and confidence. So you may ask, how does this relate to overcoming conflict in the workplace? Individuals in the workplace must get to a point where they learn to take ownership of their actions, both positive and negative. It takes a great deal of confidence and a lack of fear to reach success. The most successful and prosperous people in the world had to overcome their faults and mishaps, and move forward. There may be times when others may look at you strange, treat you differently, or develop a negative perception of you when you are involved in an embarrassing event. However, admitting to your faults and mistakes can be more helpful than not. People who take ownership of their experiences no matter how embarrassing the situation, will be able to overcome many situations dealing with conflict.

Work is a fundamental aspect of our lives; therefore we must focus on how we can consistently make it a positive experience. Why is this important? Well, mainly because work is required for most of us and it's a place where we spend a great deal of time and engage in daily responsibilities. It's crucial that we strive for satisfaction in a place where we commit much of our time. Changing our mindset to a positive one will be the first step to appreciating how we work, where we work, and what we do. Balance between work and life helps reduce stress and makes our life simple and manageable.

Outscoring conflict in the workplace is about having an attitude that enables us to face and defeat conflict and challenges. These challenges could be personal and/or work-related, but it's all about our level of confidence and how we manage our attitude and behavior. Cognitive processes, behavior, and emotions play a major role in our ability to prioritize between work and life. Too many individuals have accepted that they will not be happy on their job, no matter what happens. Well, the truth is if they keep this mindset then this will certainly be the outcome. When we decide to change our perspectives of work into an exuberant one, our attitudes will also change. As a result, our behavior on and off the job will be a reflection of the attitude we've adapted.

This book discusses ways to deal with conflict in the workplace; which contributes to the issues that can positively and negatively affect how we perform. Productivity levels, performance, and attitude are the key areas that are generally measured by organizations in which we work. This applies to employees, contractors, and self-employed workers. A healthy balance between work and one's personal life is the intention, and it should be a priority to stay motivated, encouraged, and disciplined to win in the workplace. A winning mindset, winning attitude, and winning behaviors will equate to personal and professional fulfillment. With these three attributes, conflict in the workplace can no longer hinder our growth and development. Make work a fun and exciting place to be, don't be ashamed of "farting in the boardroom", and your life at work will begin to head in a direction in which you can find ultimate happiness!

Part One:

DEFINING CONFLICT

What is Conflict?

Motivational Quote of the Day

Whenever you're in conflict with someone, there is one factor that can make the difference between damaging your relationship and deepening it. That factor is attitude. ~ William James

Conflict is a disagreement between two or more parties involving a threat to one's needs, concerns, and/or interests. When conflict occurs, there is a significant misunderstanding between truth and a perceived disagreement. Individuals in conflict base their perceptions on factors related to their morals, values, acquired information, beliefs, and life experiences. Everyone is unique, and no persons are the same and will experience conflict with others at some point in their life. Conflict does not always equate to one person being right and the other wrong. All parties involved in conflict can have a true disagreement, surprisingly enough, but complex issues can make disagreements too challenging to develop a satisfactory solution.

Conflict is not avoidable because it is a part of everyday life. One must learn to adapt to and learn ways that assist with attempts to resolve problems. When you begin to realize that your perspective will not always line up with others, you can learn to recognize challenging situations. A persons' attitude towards conflict will determine how well he/she is successful with conflict resolution. There may be times when a mediator must get involved, but whatever it may take to achieve a goal during the conflict in a positive manner, is by all means necessary. Conflict will arise regardless if you want it to or not, and you can individually learn to outscore it by maintaining a positive attitude. The more experience you gain with overcoming conflict, the better you will perceive conflict.

Questions for Reflection

Conflict has a multitude of definitions and can be perceived in different ways. What is your personal definition of "conflict"?

How do you think your attitude affects how you deal with conflict?

Personal Conflict

Motivational Quote of the Day
Peace is not absence of conflict; it is the ability to handle conflict by peaceful means. ~ Ronald Reagan

Do you recall knowing the person who brought ALL of their problems to work?! Personal conflict is one that involves unresolved personal issues and can hinder productivity in the workplace. Common reasons for personal concerns may be an imbalance with work/life responsibilities, family problems, financial instability, and many others. When one's personal life is out of order in any shape or fashion, it makes it difficult to go to work and put forth their best effort. Personal concerns can initially be an internal matter but quickly form into an external issue. Workers who are experiencing unresolved issues will struggle with enjoying their work easily. The stress that comes as a result of personal problems can escalate the level of stress that impacts work duties. Situations that are normally easy to handle will become more challenging, but it is a lack of conflict resolution that is the cause of the increased challenges.

Cognitive process, attitudes, and behaviors are influenced by personal conflict. The normal thought process can begin to take a different direction and negative emotions can evolve. One of the ways to resolve this problem is to acknowledge it, determine how the issues can be eliminated or resolved, and take action. Taking action enables individuals to face their matters and deal with it before it becomes crucial. When conflict is handled in a timely manner, individuals have the ability to enter the workplace and leave their personal issues outside. Repeated behavior and actions towards resolving this type of conflict helps prevent issues in the workplace. Determining the cause and dealing with the root issue is the beginning to finding solutions. The more workers are able to overcome personal conflict, will determine their ability to improve the dynamics of work life.

Question for Reflection

What changes in behavior do you notice when you or your colleagues are experiencing personal conflict at work?

Workplace Conflict

Motivational Quote of the Day
Conflict cannot survive without your participation ~ Wayne Dyer

When there is a problem at work, who do you call? Workplace conflict occurs when there are disagreements between two or more coworkers. Conflict in the workplace is extremely common and can be expected in almost every type of work setting involving more than one person. It can have negative effects on the performance levels of workers; therefore there must be a channel of conflict resolution present to avoid these issues. When employees are facing issues at work, they are typically facing a situation that is not in their favor. In some cases, they may find it difficult to address their concerns due to a lack of support. When this happens, workers expectations of having their needs met will diminish. Support is necessary in the workplace; otherwise there is a great potential for loss of productivity, high employee turnover, and high levels of stress and anxiety.

Why is the resolution of workplace conflict important? Well, there are many serious matters that can arise as a result. Mental health and stress are impacted; litigation issues can arise; employee turnover can be costly; and wasted time and energy will have unfavorable results. In a nutshell, good outcomes are unlikely when workplace controversy goes unresolved. Companies that focus on conflict resolution and have a high regard for their employees typically have workers who thrive and embrace conflict. This is because they are satisfied with the measures taken to handle the problems as they develop. Workplace conflict can be used as an opportunity for development and creativity, if there is an effective conflict resolution process in place.

Questions for Reflection

How do you think workplace conflict can have a negative impact on an organization?

How do you think workplace conflict can have a positive impact on an organization?

Conflict Management

Can you manage your own problems at work or is help needed?
Conflict management is the process of managing conflict in a
way that changes invalidating circumstances into positive
experiences. An advantage of going through challenging
situations is to gain knowledge, develop new perspectives, and
become open to the differences of others. It becomes a learning
experience that changes how you think, feel, and behave. In order
to make sense of something, it is acceptable to agree to disagree
with others. What's most important is to understand why others
do what they do and think how they think. In other words, it is
acceptable to compromise on differences during the argument.

Conflict management is a skill that can be taught and
generally consists of interpersonal negotiation skills. The purpose
of this skill is to encourage individuals to manage conflict on

their own for future circumstances. The better we are able to manage conflict independently, the more power we have to defeat the issue when it shows up. Conflict resolution techniques such as problem solving, learning to compromise, and managing our emotions helps us develop a win/win approach. In addition, communication helps build rapport, as well as, effective listening. The listening process helps build an understanding that will aid in the conflict management process. Most importantly, conflict management decreases stress levels, helps build working and personal relationships, and prevents future problems with others.

Questions for Reflection

List several strategies that have proven effective in resolving conflict and has helped reached a mutually satisfactory solution.

What are some skills that you could learn through conflict management that could help you establish positive outcomes during conflict with others?

Symptoms of Conflict

Can you tell when someone is going through it at work? Unresolved conflict can result in symptoms that are detrimental to an individual's feelings, self-confidence, and behaviors. In the workplace, conflict that remains unresolved can be costly and devastating. There is a negative impact on all parties involved and work morale can quickly diminish. The problem must be dealt with in a satisfactory manner in order to avoid the symptoms that appear afterwards.

Some of the symptoms that are common include stress/anxiety; unhealthy work relationships; absenteeism; loss of revenue; and mental health issues. Some of these symptoms are noticeable while others will go unnoticed by colleagues and managers. However, as the level of stress increases and problems pile up; the ability to produce results and perform exceptionally will be challenging. It is difficult to exceed performance goals under heavy loads of stress, or when we are not getting along with others. Low performance levels have a costly impact on the business. In fact, when employees experience symptoms of unresolved conflict, they can become more inclined to call off work and/or take an extended leave of absence. Depending on the severity of the problem, resignation may occur for those who find the stress to be unbearable. The goal is to take control of those symptoms as they develop so that domino effects of unforeseen issues will not begin. Taking one day at a time and having control over how we think and act are imperative to combatting the symptoms of conflict. We must be courageous in taking our work seriously without allowing the issues to burden our roles at work. Symptoms of conflict can be damaging to one's career if he/she allows them to; therefore there must be an industrious plan in place to decrease conflict-related stresses.

Question for Reflection

What advice would you give a friend or colleague who is deciding to resign from a job they once enjoyed, as a result of unresolved conflict?

Acceptable Behavior during Conflict

Motivational Quote of the Day
The successful person has unusual skill at dealing with conflict and ensuring the best outcome for all. ~ Zen Proverb

Do you feel others have a right to judge what acceptable behavior is and what is not, during conflict? The way individuals behave and react to conflict will predict the success of the outcome. Acceptable behavior during conflict begins with being a good listener. In the workplace, employees will be given the opportunity to provide suggestions on a particular task or project. The expectation is a variety of suggestions and different opinions will be presented. As employees learn to listen to one another; it will be easier for them to work collectively as a team. Danger comes when there are employees who are not good listeners and do not value the opinions of others. The next acceptable behavior involves asking for clarification. If, at any time, there is a misunderstanding, questions should be asked. Employees who do not receive clarification of why a suggestion was made can easily become confused and frustrated with the outcome. Organizations that welcome the input of their employees will typically make it feasible for them to address their concerns.

Being a team player and supporting others are also acceptable behaviors to adopt. Conflict can be a learning opportunity when you begin to think of it as a way of allowing others the chance to put their ideas to work. It can be a humbling experience when you allow others to use their creativity and develop new ideas. In some cases, you may have the greatest suggestions, but it just may not be the time to implement that plan. As employees learn to maintain humility and disengage from aggressiveness towards others, behavior during conflict will be categorized as acceptable.

Questions for Reflection

When you read about acceptable behavior in this section, what are some behaviors that you may add to this that will be helpful during conflict?

What are some actions you would take when you are working closely with others who do not exhibit acceptable behavior?

Unacceptable Behavior during Conflict

Motivational Quote of the Day
Avoid fight or flight, talk through differences. ~ Stephen Covey

When you are in conflict, there's no way your behavior will be unacceptable, right? It seems that most would know what unacceptable behavior in the workplace is; however during conflict individuals are capable of engaging in behavior that they did not intend. Emotions can get involved, and as they are integrated into conversation; words may not flow as nicely as one would have liked. This pertains to face-to-face and email conversations. It is especially important to be mindful of the tone that is conducted in an email message because it is not a favorable source of communication during conflict. Wording in an email can take the subject matter in a different direction. Employees can be accused of being too direct, too cold, and/or not personable communicating via email. The best way to communicate, if possible, while in a dispute with others at work is simply by picking up the phone or scheduling a face-to-face meeting. In fact, conflict can be avoided in some cases if personable interaction and one-on-one meetings take place while discussing a serious matter. Talking through the differences will help eliminate confusion and keep the subject matter balanced.

Unacceptable behavior includes aggressive and opposing language (verbal and body), interrupting others, and not participating in active listening. Ignoring others is also unacceptable because, at the end of the day, there is still a job that needs to be done. When employees ignore each other, they are not working as a team, and they begin to develop a negative working environment. Avoiding this type of behavior during conflict is a self-management process and it is important to change any disproving behaviors. Unacceptable behavior has never been and will never be the solution!

Questions for Reflection

What types of unacceptable behaviors have you engaged in or witnessed at work?

What are some of the consequences that you are aware of that result from unacceptable behavior during conflict?

Can Conflict Be Healthy for Work?

Motivational Quote of the Day

Difficulties are meant to rouse, not discourage. The human spirit is to grow strong by conflict. ~ William Ellery Channing

Conflict consists of disagreements, disgruntled workers, negative emotions, and undesirable behaviors; so how can it be healthy? When two or more people are in disagreement and share different perspectives, it does not always equate to a bad outcome. The healthy aspect of conflict is the ability to remain calm under pressure, becoming an active listener and gaining humility. Learning to accept the differences of others is also a healthy skill that can benefit individuals in their future dealings with people. Conflict does not always have to create tension that causes one to avoid it altogether. It should be a stepping stone to developing the strength to deal with others during challenging situations. If conflict is not resolved with effective solutions in the workplace, then employees will become discouraged to move forward when issues evolve.

In order to ensure conflict is healthy in the workplace, there must be individuals who are trained or efficient with conflict management. These individuals could include managers, team leads, Human Resource professionals, and business owners. Although these persons can delegate tasks and responsibilities to reduce problems, it is important for individuals to learn to manage conflict independently. There will not always be a time where someone else can intervene during tough situations; which explain why employees must adapt habits that are conducive to problem-solving. Adopting a positive attitude is imperative to making conflict a healthy experience. All situations do not lead to a desirable outcome, but to think of conflict as an opportunity to grow and learn is the progression to creating a healthy work environment.

Questions for Reflection

What are some ways that you can benefit from conflict?

When understanding how conflict can be healthy, what advice would you give someone who has a negative outlook on conflict?

Embrace or Avoid Conflict?

Motivational Quote of the Day

By blaming others, we fail to find the real solutions to our problems and we do not carry out our own responsibilities. ~ Jeb Bush

Why should anyone embrace conflict; which can potentially lead to more problems? Avoiding conflict sounds like the best way to deal with it as a whole, but in retrospect, everyone will face conflict at some point in our lives. Expecting conflict is a realistic approach to dealing with it, because it WILL come. So, if one knows that conflict will come sooner or later, he/she must learn to embrace it upon arrival. Embracing conflict does not mean looking for it, speaking it into existence, or having it on your mind every day. To embrace conflict means to understand the consequences of managing it effectively. Resources and professionals are available to help those who are in need of assistance. Counselors, religious leaders, consultants and trusted friends/family members are individuals outside of work who can help others with experiencing trials and tribulation.

The purpose of embracing conflict is to respect others; accept diversity; build communication abilities, and learn to value different perspectives. If these areas are mastered; it becomes easier to effectively resolve conflict in some of the most difficult situations. Learning to embrace conflict helps avoid the arguments, bickering, and heightened anger that unresolved issues can cause. It also contributes to the alleviation of stress in one's life. People who have learned to embrace challenge, tend to have lower stress levels than most. It helps give a powerful edge to avoid defeat, and this does not necessarily mean to win the argument. Embracing conflict assists with developing a winning mindset and attitude, regardless of its condition.

Questions for Reflection

What are your thoughts in regards to avoiding and embracing conflict? Which do you prefer and why?

What is your perception of embracing conflict; what does it entail?

Dangers of Conflict

Have you experienced or witnessed a situation where you or a coworker became physically, mentally, and emotionally drained by conflict at work? Dangers of conflict are related to our mental health, cognitive processes, and behaviors. The goal of conflict resolution is to reduce stress, increase analytical thinking skills, and engage in positive behavior towards others. When one is proactive in finding ways to reduce and overcome conflict, he/she is a step ahead of the other individuals involved. Avoiding the dangers of conflict can save a worker's stress load and in some cases, save the jobs of those who usually are overwhelmed at work. The purpose of being aware of the dangers of conflict is to avoid the serious dangers which are the physical and mental effects that can occur as a result of unresolved conflict. Taking control over one's own thoughts, actions, and behaviors prevents undesirable feelings and behaviors. Opportunity must be sought after in several areas; goal-setting, development of interpersonal skills, and creating peace in the work environment.

Workers who are not accustomed to opposing ideas and diversity will learn the importance of being accommodating to others. Lack of cooperating with others can result in regrets, resentment, and destructive work relationships. These consequences create mental tension, high stress levels, and inability to think clearly. When mental and physical abilities are hindered, individuals begin to deteriorate in their work. The danger involved with this is the inability to conduct business, increase productivity, and become an asset to the organization. If this happens, individuals achieve nothing and have done more harm than good. The objective is to turn conflict around before it becomes detrimental to the success of the organization.

Questions for Reflection

What common types of conflict have you experienced/witnessed that are dangerous to the growth of an organization?

What do you think are the "dangers" of ignoring conflict?

Part Two:

COMMON CONFLICT AREAS

Leadership Issues

Motivational Quote of the Day

Leadership is the art of getting someone else to do something you want done because he wants to do it. ~ Dwight D. Eisenhower

A good leader sets the tone for the attitude and actions of his/her followers. In the workplace, leaders must understand how their thought processes, decisions, and behaviors impact their followers. Workers can be positively or negatively affected by the decisions of leaders; therefore a leader must be influential. If you are a leader at work or your business, it is important to maintain a leadership style that motivates others and produces results. If you are an employee who experiences issues with those in leadership, try to find a professional way to address your concerns. There are too many talented and knowledgeable employees that are hesitant when it comes to speaking their concerns with leadership. Individuals who hold leadership positions are often given a host of responsibilities and workloads. There just may be an area that they have given little attention to that needs to be addressed. You, as a loyal employee, must take the step and bring it to his/her attention. You can request to schedule a time to speak with him/her or bring up your concerns during a meeting. Also, if there is a suggestion box, this would be a great time to include yours.

Some work settings are very small, and there may not be a traditional way of addressing concerns to leaders. It may make you feel uncomfortable, and you may develop concerns about your job status, if you were to take action. In this case, find ways to bring up the issues in a polite manner when given the opportunity to speak with him/her one on one. No matter where you work, there should always be a way to get through to management. Leaders must have consistent training on communication, interpersonal skills, and any other skill that is conducive to being an effective leader.

Business success is dependent on effective leadership, and if there are issues in this area, it can have a negative impact on revenue and profits. Workers in a business are affected when there are bad leaders or leadership behaviors. It is imperative that if you are a leader that sees a need for change, begin taking

action. If you are an employee and see a need for change, take the

necessary steps to address it.

Questions for Reflection

What are some qualities you think are required to be an effective leader?

How will you overcome challenges that you may have with individuals in leadership?

Management Styles

Motivational Quote of the Day

Good management is the art of making problems so interesting and their solutions so constructive that everyone wants to get to work and deal with them. ~ Paul Hawken

Have you experienced working with someone who had poor management skills? Management styles vary depending on the individual's personality, experience, and situation. It is important for managers to understand how their style will influence an employee's behaviors. It is normal for a team of managers to take various approaches and do things differently from one another. Some employees may find it easier to go to one manager for a particular issue and another manager for a different situation. It really depends on the style the manager has that will determine if he/she is most effective in handling a particular task/situation. One style of management that employees don't want is "bad"! There are individuals who are in management positions, but they are not approachable; friendly, or understanding of others. It is up to higher levels of management to make sure other managers are qualified to maintain their position. Poor management can cause good employees to leave the organization. They can also cause conflict with customers and this will eventually have a negative effect on the success of the business.

Two common management styles that managers may possess are autocratic and permissive. Generally, the autocratic management style is one that makes his/her decisions unilaterally. In some situations, this may work, especially when there are issues with producing a final decision amongst employees. A manager should be qualified to make strategic and effective decisions with or without a group. However, there should be a positive and favorable outcome in regards to the goals of the organization. The permissive management style is when the manager allows others to participate in the decision-making process. This type of manager is favored by employees because they feel as if their opinions and suggestions are valued. Employees love to see change and know that they played a major part in it. When managers have effective management styles, employees do their best work. If there are managers who are not effective, make sure this behavior is not ignored. It will make the entire workplace a better place to be; no matter what management style they have. Managers must do their best to use the management style that yields positive actions and results.

Questions for Reflection

What are some management styles you've known to be the most effective?

How do you deal with individuals who have poor management skills?

Employee Appreciation or Lack Thereof?

Motivational Quote of the Day

Appreciation can make a day, even change a life. Your willingness to put it into words is all that is necessary. ~ Margaret Cousins

Everyone loves to feel appreciated for their hard work and efforts on the job. Why? Well, it is very unlikely that someone wants to do good work and not be recognized for it. The most successful businesses are those that value their employee's dedication and commitment. Organizations are profitable as a result of employee's hard work; therefore they deserve the praise and recognition. Although all organizations should not be oblivious to this fact; the unfortunate fact is some of them are. There are some businesses that consist of owners and managers who do not take the time to appreciate their employees. It's difficult to think of reasons why they would do this, but according to research some have said it is costly; time consuming; and unnecessary. Many businesses that do not utilize their resources and show regard for their employee's experiences high turnovers. The lack of employee appreciation causes internal and external conflict in the workplace.

It has been proven that close to 35% of workers believe that a lack of employee appreciation hinders their performance and productivity levels. Employees resign from their companies when they are not recognized on a regular basis. Good employees at that! A lack of employee appreciation can cause stress, job dissatisfaction and is certainly a de-motivator. Although everyone is motivated by different sources, employee recognition has and will always be a major source of motivation. Performance appraisals and reviews present a good opportunity for employees to receive recognition on previous tasks and projects. Meeting and award ceremonies are also highly regarded in the workplace as a means of motivation. Employee appreciation is a morale booster, and when it is given to those who deserve it, productivity levels are almost guaranteed to increase. It is vital for companies to understand that there will always be conflict in the workplace when employees do not feel valued. If you are an employee who is a diligent worker and your manager or organization doesn't recognize it, it's time to make some suggestions for change.

Remember, sometimes change does not occur until your voice is

heard. You must always feel appreciated for excelling in your

work!

Questions for Reflection

Have you worked for someone and did not feel appreciated? If so, how did you handle it?

What are some things you would suggest an organization do, to begin recognizing their employee's efforts?

Clashing Personalities

Motivational Quote of the Day

If you are not yourself, if you surrender your personality, you have nothing left to give to the world. You have no pleasure, no use, nothing which will attract and charm me, for by the suppression of your individuality, you lose your distinctive character. ~ Edward Wilmot Blyden

Can you handle dealing with people with strong or clashing personalities? Personality clashes are extremely uncomfortable at work and can cause a great deal of stress. One of the reasons why it's so stressful is the fact that, you have to work under this circumstance daily. So, the only way to manage the situation is to find ways to deal with it. In some cases, the personality that you are clashing with can be a manager or it can be a co-worker with whom you work closely with every day. Just remember, no matter where you work there is a good chance you will have challenges with at least one person. Personality clashes can cause constant disagreement, uneasiness and can hinder the effectiveness of teamwork. It is certainly a way to create conflict and can cause individuals to lose concentration and focus on positive outcomes. It is a distraction to go to work thinking about how you need to deal with a person rather than how you are going to fulfill your work day. Depending on the person, some people can work without their performance being affected under this circumstance. However, there are people who find it very difficult and their performance levels decline.

One of the ways to resolve conflict when dealing with clashing personalities is to determine how you can still work effectively with this person. If this seems impossible, find out an appropriate time and place to discuss the matter with them. It is important to remain polite and professional during this conversation. Frustration and anger can easily show up through words; so it's imperative to remain calm. In some cases, two individuals can learn to agree to disagree. It is okay to have an understanding that the two personalities are different, but work together to develop a plan on how to work effectively. If this step is unsuccessful and communication is not healthy to sustain a positive working relationship; it may be necessary to get the right people involved. Human resources and management are usually the best groups to involve when dealing with this situation. Always choose the option that is in favor with saving your job and producing a desirable outcome for you and the other employee(s). Do not let clashing personalities get in the way of doing your best in your work!

Questions for Reflection

How does working with others with clashing personalities affect your performance?

What are some things you will do to overcome this challenge?

Work as a Team! Or Not?

Motivational Quote of the Day
Coming together is a beginning. Keeping together is progress. Working together is success. ~ Henry Ford

Have you worked on a team and had a difficult time coming to an agreement? The work environment will at some point have you working independently and as a team. Some individuals, depending on their personality, prefer to work alone, while others thrive when placed in a team. There can be advantages and disadvantages for both; however an effective worker must be able to work in both settings. Working independently can pose problems, if support is needed and a substantial amount of time is required to find support. Independent work can sometimes pose difficult situations when there are a great number of tasks/projects to be completed and no one is there to assist. In this case, there is an emergency call for teamwork to implement change and get the job done. Teamwork is common in companies and essential for accomplishing both short-term and long-term goals. However, conflict can occur with teamwork and productivity can decrease if it is not managed well. When individuals work as a team, there are a host of ideas that are compared and contrasted. Values and interests vary as well; therefore individuals engaged in teamwork must learn how to manage those differences.

When there are issues with working as a team, it is important for all members to understand what the issue is and the cause. If all team members agree there is a problem, there will be action steps taken to create a solution. All team members need to be given the opportunity to speak on how they feel it should be resolved. Determine the desirable outcome and work on a plan to reach it. The team can begin to implement the plan and find an area of compromise. Not everyone will be in agreement with the majority. The outcome has to correlate with the final goal, and if it does, you all have succeeded as a team. If a team can resolve internal conflict on its own, then they will find it less challenging to work together on accomplishing other goals. Teamwork makes the dream work, so believe in it, and you will always win while working with others.

Questions for Reflection

What are some skills you have developed during your experience of working with a team?

How do you handle conflict when working with team members who are unwilling to cooperate?

Overwhelmed with Work

Motivational Quote of the Day

Finish each day and be done with it. You have done what you could; some blunders and absurdities have crept in, forget them as soon as you can. Tomorrow is a new day; you shall begin it serenely and with too high a spirit to be encumbered with your old nonsense. ~ Ralph Waldo Emerson

Is your workload out of control? When you become overwhelmed at work, this simply means you are taking on more tasks and responsibilities than you can handle. There comes a time where you just have to slow down and analyze our workload. Time management is essential to determining how you can manage your work into increments of time. Some of those increments of time need to include downtime! Work is important, but it should not be to the point where you are not giving yourself time to clear your mind. Sometimes you may have to walk away from the desk for a little while or end your day a little early, if possible. Whatever is necessary for you to be able to come back to your work and feel refreshed and ready to give your all; make it happen. There will be days where you have to meet deadlines, and realistically there is no time for downtime. Some individuals have worked jobs that did not allow time to take much of a break. To compensate for this, one should find special downtime after work or on an off day.

It is important to maintain a positive mindset when approaching challenging and time consuming tasks. You must think of the reason why you are performing those tasks, as well as the outcome. Your attitude will determine the level of frustration you might develop when feeling overwhelmed. If you go into work with a winning attitude, you will mentally prepare yourself for the challenge. Taking care of your mental state is the first step in managing stress levels at work. You do not want to get to a place in your mind where you do not want to work. If this happens, everything will do downhill from there. Your commitment, productivity levels, and job satisfaction will decline if you allow your feelings of being overwhelmed to get in the way.

Prioritizing your tasks, creating a balance between work and free time, and acknowledging what you are capable of doing are three ways to avoid feeling overwhelmed at work. When you have demands outside of work such as family and social life, high demands at work can be extremely stressful. You need to take control of your responsibilities at work and don't allow work to control you. As you value your time, deadlines, and need for balance in your workload; you can begin to take the necessary steps to eliminate frustration and high levels of stress. You can learn to ask for assistance and/or communicate to upper management when you are unable to complete particular tasks. The intent is to get the job done in a timely manner with or without help. The goal is to make it known when assistance is needed and collectively work hard to complete all designated tasks successfully. When you are not overwhelmed at work, you enjoy it more and produce better results.

Question for Reflection

What are some things you do when you begin to feel overwhelmed with your workload?

Control Alert!

Motivational Quote of the Day

There are two kinds of people, those who do work and those who take the credit. Try to be in the first group; there is less competition there. ~ Indira Gandhi

Have you worked with individuals who try hard to be in control to the point where it causes confusion? Many individuals are placed in leadership positions, because of their ability to manage others with success. However, there are some who hold these positions, but take their controlling power to an unacceptable level. Employees who work under these types of leaders find themselves stressed, frustrated, and unwilling to follow their lead. No mature adult wants to be led by someone who decides to control people rather than focus on the agenda at hand. It is important that individuals who are "control freaks" be confronted about this unacceptable leadership style. When employees are working under this type of supervision, their only focus will be negative tension. Yes, it's important for employees to understand who is in control. However, people should never take advantage when they have the ability and/or power to manage others and particular tasks.

There are also times when there are employees who are controlling towards their counterparts. Controlling behaviors can involve compulsive behaviors, perfectionism, and the strong desire to have things go their way. The truth is, regardless of how much someone knows, employees do not want to work with or be managed by control freaks! It places everyone in an uncomfortable position and creates an undesirable work environment. Productivity can be high in some cases when employees feel their jobs are threatened by individuals in control. However, these employees will develop resentment towards the person and/or the employer quickly. High turnover rates can be a negative result of an organization with employees who are managed by extremely controlling individuals or micromanagers.

It is imperative that those who have managing power possess good qualities in the areas of communication, leadership, and management. They must recognize that although they have control over particular aspects of the work environment; they do not control people. They manage people. They manage them to be more effective in their job tasks and help them set goals. For individuals who do not hold leadership positions, but desire to be in control; they must be informed or reminded of their responsibilities. It should be brought to higher management's attention when there are individuals who try to control other employees with no authority. If managing others is not done in a professional manner, then it must be eliminated altogether. So, who's in control? You are in control of your thought processes, attitude, and behavior in the workplace. Others are not to control you, but can guide and manage you in a positive direction. Conflict will be eliminated in this area as everyone learns how to protect themselves from controlling individuals.

Question for Reflection

What are some ways you have learned to deal with controlling individuals at work?

Personal Problems and Work

Motivational Quote of the Day

If you wish to achieve worthwhile things in your personal and career life, you must become a worthwhile person in your own self-development. ~ Brian Tracy

Personal problems and work do not work together and does not produce positive results. Personal problems will bring you down emotionally and mentally. In most cases, it can affect you physically. If you go to work with the weight of your personal issues on your shoulders, you are emotionally and mentally draining your ability to perform well on the job. You should be able to go to work with a clean slate every day and push your problems to the side. Co-workers are not always the best individuals to talk to about your problems. Why? They are not counselors or psychologists, and although you may have developed a friendship with many of them; work is not the place to discuss personal issues. There are several problems that can stem from this. Attention that should be given to your job duties is now directed on addressing your problems to your counterparts. If they are listening to you, then they are also being taken away from what they are supposed to be doing. When you lose time at work, you lose productivity. If you lose productivity, then the organization suffers.

Leaving your personal problems outside of work will benefit you, your co-workers, and the organization as a whole. It is important to seek help for personal problems that have become a disturbance to how you think and behave at work. Some organizations have an employee assistance line for those who have a difficult time maintaining balance between their life and work. If you or someone you know is experiencing these issues, this is a great suggestion to help them cope. Some employees have mentioned their experience of working with people who mentally drained them with their dreadful problems every day! This is annoying, and you will get to a point where you don't want to be in their presence. However, if you are required to complete a task or project with them; then you are forced to hear their problems. This shouldn't be acceptable in the workplace. In some cases, you may have to take a stand and inform the person in a professional manner that you would prefer to direct your focus on the job rather than having personal conversations. Some workers have had to do this, and although it is difficult to say, it makes a huge difference in your working relationship. You will be able to focus, as well as the other person, and your performance levels will not be hindered. Personal problems must be handled discreetly, and the only individuals at work that should be informed are management, if necessary. The goal is to avoid conflict by avoiding addressing personal issues at work. It will allow employees to focus on the job and create a productive work environment.

Question for Reflection

What are some ways that you would maintain balance between personal issues and work?

Is Your Voice Heard?

Motivational Quote of the Day
What you do speaks so loudly that I cannot hear what you say. ~ Ralph Waldo Emerson

Have you had a hard time getting your voice heard when you have concerns at work? Many people complain about how they have issues with certain policies and other areas of conflict that goes unresolved. The reason they say it remains an issue is because they are being ignored by management and leadership in the organization. This can be a major issue in the workplace because employees should have the right to voice their opinions and offer suggestions when needed. Businesses, rather small or large, should have an open door policy that allows their employees to make suggestions for improvement. It is a defined way of learning about the problem areas that may cause a decrease in productivity and job satisfaction.

If you are a worker who is diligent and committed to the organization, you should have access to any resources that allow you to voice your opinion. When you are committed to your job, your opinion will be highly valued. Team meetings, performance appraisal time, and conferences may be the opportunity to address any concerns you may have. Sometimes you may have to schedule a one-on-one meeting with management if you don't foresee an upcoming opportunity to speak. An organization with effective management will encourage and welcome new ideas and suggestions from their employees on a regular basis. Their goal is to make the effort to listen to what is on their employee's minds. If the concerns need to involve change, they are willing to design a plan to produce change. This may take time; however it is important that organizations have an open door policy. Employees feel secure and comfortable working for someone or an organization that values their opinion. They want to feel as if they can make a contribution to the growth and development of the organization. If you are an employee who seeks change and recognize the need for improvement in a particular area, make your voice heard and expect positive results. The organization needs individuals like you who will help make a difference!

Questions for Reflection

How can you begin to make a difference in your workplace when you see areas that need improvement?

What have you found to be the best ways to make your voice heard at work?

Getting the Job Done!

Motivational Quote of the Day
The more I want to get something done, the less I call it work. ~ Richard Bach

No matter what type of work you are doing, your ultimate goal is to get the job done. What does this entail? It means to get motivated, stay motivated, and use that motivation to do the best at your job. You may have to set small goals to be able to tackle the larger ones, but in the end you must get it done. If you are an employee of a company, in management, or own your own business; your purpose is to complete your job successfully and encourage others to do so. In most cases, you need the assistance of others to handle particular tasks that you are unable to manage. This is the reason for teamwork, and you must collectively work together to accomplish goals.

One of the ways to get the job done is to make sure you are utilizing all the resources that are made available to you. This makes the process much easier and quicker to manage. Some of the resources may pertain to using new technology, current literature, delegating tasks to other employees, and making sure previous tasks are completed. It's all about having the right resources present that will enable workers to do their job effectively. A lack of resources can put a restraint on productivity and performance in the workplace. If you are not in a position to provide resources, then make suggestions on ways to make the job easier. Some smaller businesses may not have all the necessary resources available due to budget constraints and other reasons, but as a worker you must try to make the best out of what you have.

Getting the job done is motivating in itself! It is a way that you can appreciate your hard work and efforts. It is a time to reflect on why you worked so hard and encourage you to move on to the next project with ease. As workers complete their tasks, goals are being accomplished, and the business is progressing. Sometimes, it is easy to get caught up in the routine of work that you forget how your daily contributions are making a tremendous difference. Continue to do your best and get the job done!

Questions for Reflection

What are some things that will always make it easier for you to get the job done no matter where you work?

How do you think organizations can ensure their employees are consistent with meeting daily/monthly goals?

Part Three:

OUTSCORING CONFLICT AT WORK

Begin Your Day the Right Way

Motivational Quote of the Day
Time is the most valuable thing a man can spend. ~ Laertius Diogenes

What efforts do you make to ensure the rest of your day will run smooth? How you begin your day has a significant impact on your attitude and productivity level at work. You must focus on having a good start so that you are able to maintain control over any negative factors that can be a distraction. The things you do in the beginning of your day can dictate rather you will have a good or bad day. The goal is to stay committed to performing the necessary tasks that result in staying in a good mood and being productive. Some of the ways to do this is to wake up in a timely manner. Rushing can create feelings of anxiety, worry, and it immediately puts you in a distressed state. Give yourself plenty of time to get things together in the morning. It also helps to make room for some personal time such as reading or meditating before heading out. This gives a sense of calmness and tranquility; which is essential to having a peaceful state of mind.

When you take control of your time prior to work, you develop a mindset that prepares you for accomplishment for the remainder of the day. This works especially well for those times you expect a heavy workload and/or busy days. In addition to managing your time for your benefit, it leaves a lasting impression on others. Being on time is highly regarded and shows that you value what you do and respect others.

Making time to get to work early enough to organize your thoughts and create an agenda for the day is helpful. It will alleviate stress and allow you the opportunity to sort out a plan. Creating a good workspace can set a positive tone for how your day will go. If you are behind on work from previous days, this may be a time to determine when you will catch up on those tasks. If you have extra time, this will be the time to do so. The purpose of starting the day right is to ensure the day runs as smooth as possible, with minimal distractions, and less frustration. If you can make it a habit to clear your mind and make time before you start working, you are on your way to a productive and successful day.

Questions for Reflection

What are some ways you can make the most of your time to get your day off to a great start?

Are there negative habits that you need to replace with positive ones?

Believing You Can Do Your Job Well

Motivational Quote of the Day

Plenty of men can do good work for a spurt and with immediate promotion in mind, but for promotion you want a man in whom good work has become a habit. ~ Henry L. Doherty

Are you doing your best no matter how much like your job? Knowing that you are great at what you do is a process from the beginning. At first, you learn the basic tasks that are a requirement. As time progresses, you become experienced and confident in your ability to get the job done. This is the point when you believe in yourself and others begin to value your work. When your job is done effectively, it is noticed by management, clients, co-workers, etc. In other words, your performance impacts you and all the other individuals within your environment. The positive impact is the expectation that you anticipate from doing good work. When you believe you do your job well, you position yourself to train those who may need it. In many cases, individuals who excel at their work are delegated the responsibility to act as a leader. This may lead to recognition, promotions, and other forms of praise. It will all be well-deserved, for hard work always goes unnoticed. The belief that you can do your job well begins internally, and the external outcomes will eventually evolve. The internal belief enhances your character, and you begin to discover your strengths. Strengths are determined through diligent work and trial and error at times. Learning to use your strengths and become an asset to your organization is the key to successful endeavors.

Believing you can do your job well is mentally and emotionally rewarding. It helps you build a level of respect amongst your peers and counterparts. Also, your behaviors become influential, and you are able to lead by example. You are setting a tone within your work environment that motivates others to jump on the "do your job well" bandwagon. Most importantly, as you believe that you do your job well, you develop a desire to learn more and increase your level of knowledge and skill sets. As a result, you become a greater asset to your organization. You become the reason why employers and businesses experience growth and achieve their goals. Overall, you experience higher potential and growth to reach your

personal goals simply by believing that you are the best at what

you do.

Questions for Reflection

Where do you stand in regards to your performance while working?

What are some ways you can begin or continue to have a positive impact on others by performing well?

Maintaining Confidence

Motivational Quote of the Day

One important key to success is self-confidence. An important key to self-confidence is preparation. ~ Arthur Ashe

Do you believe in yourself and your ability to exceed? Confidence plays a tremendous role in your attitude, performance, ability to complete a task, and level of success. When you are confident in your work, you naturally attract others and build an impressive reputation. The key to maintaining confidence is to be the one that others listen to, respect, and want to follow. As you build your confidence in your work, you automatically possess some leadership characteristics that assure others that you know your work. Although it may be difficult to build confidence when starting a new job or project, it helps to appear to others that you are confident. This means you can pretend to be confident! You will be surprised how this influences others perceptions of you. It is a misperception that you can't be confident as you learn new things. Confidence is the ability to believe in yourself and know that you are capable of performing a task or achieving a goal. When learning new information or skills, you can be confident that you are a quick learner and be able to apply it to your work. Confidence allows you to demonstrate a positive attitude towards learning, teaching, and tackle any challenge that comes your way. It is your level of confidence that will be the reason why you are able to overcome challenging obstacles in your personal life and at work.

Some of the ways to maintain confidence involves speaking positive words and avoid saying the words "I can't." These words oppose confidence and hinder your vision of being able to accomplish a particular task. Making sure words you choose align with your actions will be a way to think before making decisions. When you make mistakes, be confident enough to ask others for advice and learn from them. As your confidence increases with time and experience, you will feel secure in your decision-making abilities and life choices. This can positively affect your career path and advancement. It is important to look, act, and feel confident to keep you grounded. Maintaining confidence is a choice and should become a habit that you will automatically develop as you gain knowledge. It will contribute greatly to your ability to succeed in all you do.

Questions for Reflection

What are some things you can do to boost your confidence on a daily basis?

When faced with a challenging circumstance, how do you feel confidence plays a role in your ability to overcome the situation?

Staying Loyal To Your Organization

Motivational Quote of the Day
Individual commitment to a group effort – that is what makes a team work, a company work, a society work, a civilization work.
~ Vincent Lombardi

What are you saying about your job/company outside of work?

Loyalty to an organization is important because you will take

pride and value its mission and objective. A feeling of loyalty

allows you to make a commitment to contribute your efforts

towards achieving a common purpose. When you are loyal, you

are excited about what the company has to offer, and your actions

will show it. Other individuals should recognize your loyalty by

how you speak of the company. The time you put in such as

voluntarily working extra hours to meet a goal is a demonstration

of your loyalty. Encouraging others to purchase and/use the

products and services, even outside of work, is another form of

loyalty. Loyalty gives you confidence because you believe that

you represent a business and/or organization that have a future.

Enjoying the work atmosphere and job satisfaction are results of being loyal to your company. When you are satisfied on the job, your loyalty will extend to offering suggestions for improvement in the company's operations. If you see there is a need or recognize potential in a specific area, you will find yourselves addressing those concerns. You will want to make a difference in the organization and find value in giving your input. Loyalty will open the doors for career advancement and other opportunities for management. Organizations want individuals who are committed and going to be loyal. They want employees who will do what it takes to make the company a better place to be.

Some of the direct ways to demonstrate loyalty to your organization is suggesting new and innovative ideas. You never know if your idea will become a major concentration area for development. Another way is to volunteer to participate in groups or projects that will improve the image or goal of the company. Volunteering your time is an excellent way to show that you place great emphasis on valuing your organization. When you stay loyal to your organization, you are creating a connection between your commitment and your happiness. It is a good place to be when you are determined to be an asset to your

organization.

Questions for Reflection

How have you demonstrated loyalty to your organization?

Has your loyalty to your organization had an impact on your level of happiness at work?

Understanding Your Role

Motivational Quote of the Day

*Your work is to discover your world and then with all your heart
to give yourself to it. ~ Buddha*

Do you focus heavily on your role or your purpose? Your role at
work goes beyond your job description and basic duties. If you
vision how you can be the best at what you do, then your role
becomes more than just a set of duties. Your role becomes an
opportunity for you to develop self-awareness and find ways to
nurture it. It is helpful to determine your level of contribution to
your role and the impact it has on the internal and external
environment. Internal environment involves all of the factors at
work such as change, direction of the company, and planning that
affects your role either directly or indirectly. External
environment pertains to your load of responsibilities outside of
work that determines how much you can mentally give. For
example, if you have major responsibilities such as family,
education, and other obligations outside of work; you may find it
difficult to commit extra time to your job. In this case, you would

use your time wisely and utilize any resources that are made available to you while you are working. Another way to understand your role thoroughly is to participate in training that can enhance your skill set and ability to become more effective. It is never a time when you can gain too much information, even if you have to retake a course that is applicable to your position. It is beneficial to refresh your memory and generate enthusiasm about performing your job. It is useful to take advantage of any educational resources such as articles, volunteer opportunities, and meetings that will give you clarity in your work.

As you analyze your background and previous work experiences, you can use the knowledge and apply it to your current role. If there are any important accomplishments that you've made, it is good to reflect on those moments. They will provide the motivation needed to reach your highest potential in your current role. Understanding your role gives you balance, confidence, and creativity to make your job/career stimulating. It is a self-development process that involves procedure, systematic processes, but most importantly effectiveness. Having an in-depth understanding of your role is a way to create sustainable

results in your growth and performance.

Questions for Reflection

What are some ways you have become more effective by understanding your role?

How have your previous work and/or educational background contributed to your current role?

Working Well With Others

Motivational Quote of the Day

It's easy to figure out who isn't a team player. They'll constantly remind the coach just how good they are. ~ Brian G. Jett

Do you work best independently or as a team? The ability to work well with others is important and is a must in order to build a foundation of productivity. This applies to employees in management and non-managerial positions, business owners, and every individual who offers a product/service. If one does not have the personality or desire to work well with others, there is almost a guarantee that he/she will not be successful. There is a need to build effective working relationships with those in your environment. It is a healthy benefit to feeling as if you have balance in your line of work. Working relationships that are healthy promotes peace, job satisfaction, and motivation. As you work with others, it is important to take as much as you can from the experience. Find out what new information or skill you can learn from them and vice versa. It is an opportunity to exchange ideas and concepts that will make the workplace a more exciting place to be.

In many situations, teamwork is an area that can be fun yet challenging for most. Teamwork requires an understanding that individuals will bring their similarities and differences together to achieve a common purpose. Diversity is a main factor when working with others because it is important to respect the differences of others. While working you may begin to realize there are some people who have different perspectives that stem from their work background and experiences. This is actually a value when working as a team. It helps to hear how a problem can be resolved hearing different perspectives in order to make sense of what it takes to come to a defined solution. When you realize working well with others is an advantage and certainly not a disadvantage, you will begin to take pride in doing so. Effective working relationships lead to desirable business opportunities; enhances communication skills; and promotes developmental skills. This type of relationship involves a great deal of respect for others, trust, and honesty. These are essentials when working with others and a lack of any of these three elements will create conflict. Working well with others is not only a requirement, but it serves as a catalyst to productive work and high performance levels.

Questions for Reflection

When working with others, how do you value the beliefs and perspectives as others when making difficult decisions?

When working as a team, what do you feel is the most important characteristic to building an effective team?

Manager-Employee Relationship

Motivational Quote of the Day
Effective leadership is putting things first. Effective management is discipline, carrying it out. ~ Stephen Covey

What is your relationship like with your employee/manager? The manager-employee relationship has a major impact on the performance of an employee. It is critical that there is a connection between the two in order to maintain employee satisfaction. When you are working as an employee, you must have confidence that your manager considers your efforts and cares about your well-being. Managers who possess good leadership skills and abilities understand individual and group goals. They will do what is necessary to meet those goals and make sure all workers are involved. As an employee, one must be willing to express their interests and concerns to his/her manager with no problems. Open communication between the two is the key to gaining a clear understanding of objectives and future expectations. When an employee feels he/she can address any concerns to management, it creates a sense of belonging to the organization. Employees work harder and more efficiently when they have open communication lines with management. Many organizations with managers, who are the least concerned with how the employees feel, generally have a high turnover rate. To enjoy your work, you must have a healthy and effective working relationship with those in management.

Managers must be great at communicating the organizational goals, changes, values, and objectives to their employees. An effective manager is open to receiving feedback from employees and considers this to be an opportunity to make any necessary changes. If you manage a business or hold a management position, it is imperative that you value the employee's opinions and determine how they can contribute to the overall success of the organization. If you are an employee, it is necessary to utilize many resources and tools that are made available to you by management. Scheduling time to speak with management on a one-on-one basis may be needed if there are issues that have not been addressed or suggestions for improvement. Simple enough, scheduling one-on-meetings with management is a good idea to build rapport and get on the path to building a good working relationship.

Questions for Reflection

What are some ways you can or have built an effective working relationship with those who you have managed or have managed you?

What are the benefits you've experienced with maintaining a good manager-employee relationship?

Find Passion in Working

Motivational Quote of the Day
When love and skill work together, expect a masterpiece. ~ John Ruskin

Do you think you can find passion working in a job you love, as well as one you dislike? Passion in working promotes self-development, awareness, and growth. It is a drive to succeed at any task that comes your way. With passion, you have an internal desire to get the job done and take pride in the journey trying to accomplish your goals. If your current job or line of work is not what you dreamed of, it is important to understand the reasons why you work. When the "why" is defined one will tend to take his/her work seriously and become the best at it. You want to take ownership of your projects and lead it out to its completion. Your passion becomes like fuel, and it influences the workers around you. It is admired by most, and co-workers, managers, clients, etc. appreciate the passion. It doesn't matter if you have an entry level position, management position, CEO, or even a volunteer; passion is exciting. It makes a difference in your attitude towards doing your work. You develop a winning attitude that will allow room for you to distort any negative factors that are a disruption to your work. Overcoming challenges are less difficult when passion is involved; your approach to resolving problems is handled with diligence. Winners always win, because they see and feel the value of the outcome. Winning in the workplace begins with finding passion in what you do.

It is the passion in working that causes you to be innovative and determined to try different approaches to accomplish a goal. You become adaptive to change and be prepared for modifying what is necessary to resolve a problem. As you all know, problems with work will come. It is a matter of using the fuel of your passion to develop your critical thinking skills. When there is a lack of passion, you are less likely to go the extra mile while working. Without passion, businesses would fail, and strategic planning would go downhill. When you begin to understand the benefit in having passion, even when it is not a dream job, you can appreciate what it takes to be an excellent worker. Having passion when working for someone else helps you to develop the

skills and drive to get to a point where you want to be in the
future. To get optimal results in working, you must have passion.

Questions for Reflection

What are some ways you think having passion can or has made a difference in how you feel about your work?

How do you think your passion can influence those around you?

Effective Communication

How are your words and tone with others? Is it what you say or how you say it? Or both? Communicating effectively is extremely important when working with others. At times, it can be difficult and frustrating, but it is a skill that must be mastered. Communication involves the exchange and sharing of information between at least two or more people. It is a skill that is required to maintain positive personal and business relationships. Achieving goals, getting tasks completed, and creating a level of understanding is constructive for communication. Without effective communication, conflict can easily become an issue. Conflict usually occurs due to a lack of compromise or ineffective communication. To avoid conflict, workers must learn to master their communication skills; even if this requires a course on the subject. Organizations have offered training and workshops that are built around effective communication. It is essential that all working individuals value this skill because it can be a making or breaking point in their career. If a business owner does not engage in effective communication, his/her employees can withdraw and lose satisfaction in their jobs. If employees do not communicate effectively with their managers, there will be a constant flow of misunderstanding and frustration. It is imperative that communication remains a priority for organizations, as well as individuals who have businesses where they work alone.

Effective communication allows for better coordination for tasks, meetings, and goal-setting. It also helps maintain good working relationships between employees and managers, self-employed and clients, and employees and customers. An open line of communication gives everyone a higher level of comfort and trust in the organization in which he/she works. Some of the ways to improve effective communication are being precise in discussing particular matters, preparation, and being an excellent listener. Communication is a two-way process; therefore both parties should send a message to one another. Effective

communication is the key to great decision-making skills;

problem solving, and building trust in others.

Questions for Reflection

What are some ways you can see positive results by engaging in effective communication?

How do you handle situations when there is ineffective communication in the workplace?

Overcoming Conflict at Work

Motivational Quote of the Day

Conflicts may be the sources of defeat, lost life, and a limitation of our potentiality but they may also lead to greater depth of living and the birth of more far-reaching unities, which flourish in the tensions that engender them. ~ Karl Jasper

Get over the problems at work and move forward! Conflict in the workplace is something you want to avoid at all costs; however it is not about "if" it will occur, it is "when" it will occur. Conflict can pertain to communication issues, interacting with others, policy issues, and mismatched values. It is likely to happen anywhere that you work. How you handle conflict and the ability to maintain a positive attitude will determine if you can overcome it. Your attitude takes precedence over any circumstance you face. You must develop an attitude that says you can win no matter what comes our way. Obtaining access to many resources can help you overcome obstacles you face on and off the job. You must take advantage of resources for your benefit because you don't want to feel defeated, even when the odds are against you. It is up to you to determine how to resolve problems before they create more issues.

Identifying the problem and communicating it to the appropriate persons involved are two ways to overcome conflict. While communicating, it is imperative that everyone's voice is heard, and all persons involved are listening to one another. When there is conflict, there are generally several points of views to analyze. The next step is to develop a plan and begin brainstorming ideas for a solution. This will take time to organize and prioritize issues that need to be addressed first. After this plan is developed, it is time for implementation. The focus is to determine what solutions work best for the situation at hand. Remember, all conflict has a resolution; therefore choosing the best solution can be challenging but is worth it in the end. You can overcome conflict in a particular area and begin using this strategy for many others issues you may face, and you will find that conflict resolution is favorable. Most importantly, a plan to produce change is beneficial; however a positive attitude is the key to overcoming conflict at the workplace. While working on a plan and determining a solution, you must keep a positive attitude, maintain confidence, and continue performing well on the job. You will be successful in the end and can use this experience to help others who experience conflict in the future.

Questions for Reflection

What are some things you have done to resolve an internal conflict amongst those you've worked with?

What advice would you give to help those who struggle with conflict in the workplace?

CONCLUSION

Outscoring conflict in the workplace is critical to one's well-being and success. As organizations strive to invest in resolving conflict and develop great leaders, the business will continue to accomplish its' goals. Workers, who take time and effort to maintain healthy relationships and keep a positive attitude, will find themselves happier at work. Those who admit to "farting" in the boardroom are most likely to confront a situation and own up to their actions! Those who do not speak up when they "fart" will look around and wait for someone else to be blamed. Conflict is an issue that we will all face, and as we learn to take control and handle the situation in an effective way, we will develop the skills to minimize conflict as a whole.

The process of outscoring conflict involves the ability to turn problems around. Instead of allowing conflict to take control over your emotions and lead to high levels of stress, you can begin to turn it into an empowering event. Facing conflict is your opportunity to lead by example, stand up for your rights, and prevent past issues from reoccurring. It will take individuals that are ready to overcome conflict that will help make a difference in their organization. Those who win in the workplace are those that are great listeners, respectful of differences, and excellent communicators. The ultimate goal to outscoring conflict in the workplace is to arrive at a positive resolution in every situation. As you become active at resolving conflict, you are able to create a motivating, influential, and positive work environment for everyone. So, admit to "farting in the boardroom" and you will be the one with the strength to outscore conflict in the workplace!

ACKNOWLEDGMENTS

Thanks to my husband (for his sense of humor), parents, grandparents, and extended family members, friends, and colleagues who have supported me through my writing journey and my first book titled, "I live. I struggle. I WIN!" I also want to thank my friend and photographer, Jehan, for the beautiful photos; and make-up artist Brooklynn Carter, both from Columbus, Ohio. Thank you all for your contributions to my inspiration and knowledge for creating this book.

ABOUT THE AUTHOR

Diara Kendrich is an author, speaker, and Organizational Consultant with over 10 years of experience in Sales, Management, Consulting, and Customer Service. She holds a Bachelors of Arts in Psychology from Argosy University and earned her Masters of Science in Psychology, specializing in Industrial/Organizational Psychology, from Capella University in 2012 and graduated with Honors. Diara is the author of an inspirational book titled, "I live. I struggle. I WIN!"; published in 2011. She has received recognition for her volunteer work in conducting surveys on customer and employee feedback in the transportation industry. Her volunteer work also includes student mentoring and helping persons with disabilities. Diara has also been interviewed on various blog talk shows throughout the U.S. She has combined her work experience and educational background in her writing, with a passion to help employees take control of common conflict issues in the workplace.

CONTACT INFO:

Diara Kendrich

P.O. Box 723011

Atlanta, GA 31139

(678) 509-5251

www.dkendrich.com

www.ingramcontent.com/pod-product-compliance
Lightning Source LLC
Chambersburg PA
CBHW030903180526
45163CB00004B/1685